HISTORY CORNER

Victorians

Alice Harman

WAYLAND

Explore the world with **Popcorn** - your complete first non-fiction library.

Look out for more titles in the Popcorn range. All books have the same format of simple text and striking images. Text is carefully matched to the pictures to help readers to identify and understand key vocabulary.
www.waylandbooks.co.uk/popcorn

First published in 2012 by Wayland
Copyright © Wayland 2012

Wayland
Hachette Children's Books
338 Euston Road
London NW1 3BH

Wayland Australia
Level 17/207 Kent Street
Sydney NSW 2000

Produced for Wayland by
White-Thomson Publishing Ltd
www.wtpub.co.uk
+44 (0)843 208 7460

Editor: Alice Harman
Designer: Clare Nicholas
Picture researcher: Alice Harman
Series consultant: Kate Ruttle
Design concept: Paul Cherrill

British Library Cataloguing in Publication Data
Harman, Alice.
   Victorians. -- (History corner)(Popcorn)
   1. Great Britain--History--Victoria, 1837-1901--Juvenile
literature. 2. Great Britain--Social conditions--19th
century--Juvenile literature. 3. Great Britain--Social
life and customs--19th century--Juvenile literature.
I. Title II. Series
941'.081-dc23

ISBN: 978 0 7502 6730 4

Wayland is a division of Hachette Children's Books,
an Hachette UK company.
www.hachette.co.uk

Printed and bound in China

Picture/illustration credits: Alamy: Pictorial Press Ltd
8, Photri Images 17, Amoret Tanner 20; Peter Bull: 23;
Corbis: The Francis Frith Collection 12; Getty Images:
The Bridgeman Art Library 7, 13, 19; Mary Evans
Picture Library: 6, 14, 16, 18; Stefan Chabluk: 5 (map);
Shutterstock: Oleg Golovnev 5, photocell 12, (Inset);
Topfoto: Topham Picturepoint 15, English Heritage/HIP,
21; Wikimedia: 4

Every effort has been made to clear copyright.
Should there be any inadvertent omission,
please apply to the publisher for rectification.

Contents

Who were the Victorians?

The Victorians were people who lived in Britain when Queen Victoria ruled the country. She was Britain's queen for almost 64 years.

Queen Victoria ruled for longer than any other British king or queen.

Victoria was only 18 years old when she became queen in 1837.

This map shows the British Empire around 120 years ago. All the countries in pink were part of the empire. Victoria was queen of these countries.

Canada

United Kingdom

Aden

India

Burma

British Guiana

Gambia

Sierra Leone

Gold Coast

Nigeria

Ceylon

British East Africa

Singapore

British New Guinea

South Africa

Australia

New Zealand

Town and country

Many Victorians moved from the countryside to find work in towns and cities. City centres were often crowded and smelly.

The drinking water in cities was dirty, and made people very ill.

People had to keep out the way of horses pulling carriages through the busy streets!

Some rich families owned large farms in the countryside. Lots of people worked long hours on these farms for very little money.

Women often cared for their children while working in the fields.

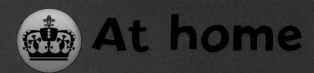

At home

Most people in cities lived in crowded areas called slums. The houses here were small, dark and dirty.

In the slums, families often shared a house. A large family would live in one or two rooms.

Rich families normally had two big houses, one in the city and another in the countryside. Rooms were decorated with furniture made of gold, silk and expensive wood.

These people are playing a game called 'Blind Man's Buff'.

9

Food and drink

Victorians bought some of their food in small shops, and some at a weekly market. Rich families sent their servants to do the shopping.

People came into town from the nearby countryside to buy and sell food at markets.

Tea was a very popular drink that was enjoyed by rich and poor people. Most people drank tea every day.

Servants were often given a small amount of tea as part of their wages.

Rich women had tea with cakes and biscuits in the afternoon.

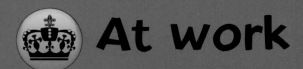

At work

Victorian men often learned to do the same job as their fathers. Most women worked in the home. Some women also had jobs, such as working in a factory.

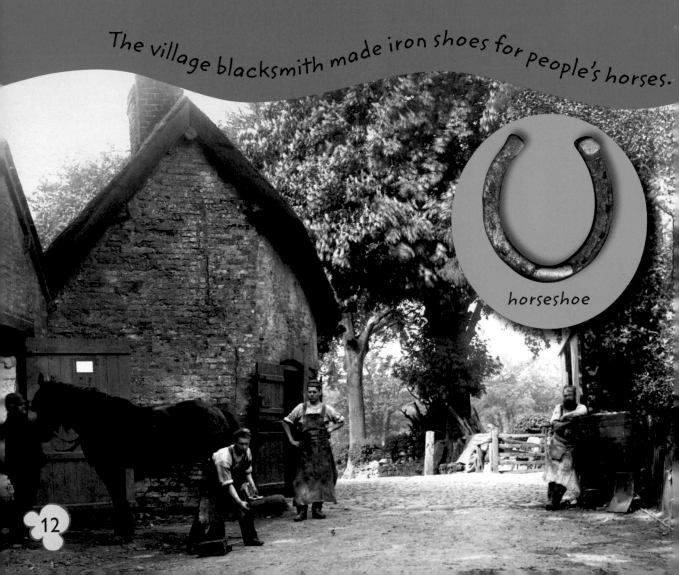

The village blacksmith made iron shoes for people's horses.

horseshoe

Many children from poor families worked in factories. The work was dangerous, and these children often got badly hurt.

These boys are working in a factory that makes cloth.

In early Victorian times, children as young as three went to work.

Clothes

Rich women wore colourful dresses with huge skirts that touched the floor. They always put on hats when they went outside.

Girls dressed like their mothers, but with shorter skirts.

Imp. Legastelois et Vanguet, r St Elizabeth 11 a Paris.

Poor people had to wear the same clothes for a long time. They mended their shoes and clothes, and tried to keep them clean.

Homeless children normally had no shoes, and walked around barefoot.

At school

Many children did not go to school, because they had to work. Some poor children went to free charity schools.

Young children often went to nearby 'Dame' schools, run by women in their homes.

Victorians teachers were very strict. If children were noisy or didn't finish their work, they were hit with a thin stick called a cane.

There were often 70 or 80 children in one class.

This class is cutting leaf shapes out of paper.

17

Toys and games

Rich children had lots of different toys and games. The most popular toys were rocking horses, doll's houses and train sets.

The man in the tall hat is treating all his lucky grandchildren to new toys!

18

Poor children played with homemade toys, such as dolls made of cloth rags. They saved money to buy skipping ropes and marbles.

These boys are playing a game of marbles, trying to knock each other's marbles out of the circle.

Poor children played in the street, where there was more space than in their homes.

Holidays and festivals

Many Christmas traditions in Britain began in Victorian times. These include decorating Christmas trees, sending cards and pulling crackers.

Queen Victoria and her husband had the first Christmas tree in Britain.

Families made tree decorations at home, and kept them for many years.

Families almost never went abroad for a summer holiday. They took the train to the seaside. People enjoyed paddling, eating ice cream and making sandcastles.

Most Victorians wore their ordinary clothes on the beach, even in the hot sun!

21

Design a postage stamp

The postage stamp was first invented in Victorian Britain. The very first stamp was called a Penny Black, and had Queen Victoria's face on it. After the Penny Black came the Penny Red, and then the Penny Lilac.

Which stamp do you think is which?

Design your own postage stamp! Draw a rectangle shape, with a big picture in the middle. Decorate the sides and corners of the stamp with patterns. Colour your stamp in, and don't forget to include the price on the stamp.

Make a cornucopia

Cornucopias were popular Christmas tree decorations in Victorian times.

1. Cut the shape of this template out of a piece of card. Roll it into a cone shape. Stick down the inside edge with sticky tape.

2. Ask an adult to help you pierce holes on opposite sides of the cone.

3. Thread a piece of ribbon or string through the holes, and tie it to make a big loop.

4. Decorate the cone, and fill it with sweets, nuts or other small treats. Now hang it up on your tree!

Visit our website to download larger, printable templates for this project.
www.waylandbooks.co.uk/popcorn

Glossary

carriage a vehicle with wheels that is pulled by horses

charity money or other types of help given to people in need

cloth material made from cotton, wool or other types of thread

cracker a cardboard tube with small presents inside, which bangs when pulled apart

empire a group of countries ruled by one person

homeless describes someone who doesn't have a home to live in, and has to sleep outside

mend fix something that is broken

rags very old, torn clothes

servant a person who works in someone else's house, cooking, cleaning or looking after the home in other ways

slums a poor, crowded area of a city

strict if someone is strict, they make people obey the rules and behave in a certain way

wages money that a person is paid for doing their job

Index

EXPLORE THE WORLD WITH THE POPCORN NON-FICTION LIBRARY!

- Develops children's knowledge and understanding of the world by covering a wide range of topics in a fun, colourful and engaging way
- Simple sentence structure builds readers' confidence
- Text checked by an experienced literacy consultant and primary deputy-head teacher
- Closely matched pictures and text enable children to decode words
- Includes a cross-curricular activity in the back of each book

WATCH OUT! — ear Water — Honor Head

HISTORY CORNER — The Great Fire of London — Jenny Powell

SCIENCE CORNER — Sound and Hearing — Angela Royston

FAMILIES — My Mum — Katie Dicker

GOOD FOOD — Vegetables — Julia Adams

PEOPLE WHO HELP US — Police — Honor Head

OPLE WHO HELP US — refighters — Honor Head

GEOGRAPHY CORNER — Rainforests — Ruth Thomson

A YEAR OF FESTIVALS — Muslim Festivals — Honor Head

HISTORY CORNER — The Gunpowder Plot — Jenny Powell

IN SPACE — Planets — Chris Oxlade

SEASONS — Winter — Kay Barnham

FREE DOWNLOADS!

- Written by an experienced teacher
- Learning objectives clearly marked
- Provides information on where the books fit into the curriculum
- Photocopiable so pupils can take them home

OVER 50 TITLES TO CHOOSE FROM!

www.waylandbooks.co.uk/downloads